TO

Throws for Strikers:
The Forgotten Throws
of Karate, Boxing
and Taekwondo

By
Iain Abernethy

NETH
PUBLISHING

Published by: NETH Publishing
In association with Summersdale Publishers Ltd
www.summersdale.com
www.iainabernethy.com

Throws for Strikers: The Forgotten Throws of Karate, Boxing and Taekwondo

Copyright © Iain Abernethy 2003

1st Edition

Published by: NETH Publishing, PO Box 38, Cockermouth, CA13 0GS, UK.

In association with Summersdale Publishers Ltd, 46 West Street, Chichester, PO19 1RP, UK. www.summersdale.com

Cover illustration and photographs by Peter Skillen

Typesetting by My Word!, 138 Railway Terrace, Rugby, Warkwickshire CV21 3HN.

Printed and bound in Great Britain by Bookcraft (Bath) Ltd, Midsomer Norton, Somerset.

A CIP Catalogue record for this book is available from the British Library.

ISBN: 0 9538932 2 7

Important note: The author, publishers and distributors of this book do not accept any responsibility for any prosecutions or proceedings brought or instituted against any person or body as a result of the use or misuse of the information or any techniques described in this book or any loss, injury or damage caused thereby. Some of the techniques and training methods described in this book require high levels of skill and physical fitness. The techniques and methods described within this book must only be practised by those in good health whilst under qualified supervision.

Acknowledgements

As I sat down to write these acknowledgements (thank you for not skipping past them by the way), it occurred to me that it would be possible to save a little time by 'cutting and pasting' the acknowledgements from my previous books! Not that I ever would, but it does show how supportive everyone has been when I find myself thanking the same people time after time. Their continued support means a great deal to me. If it weren't for their kindness and generosity this book would never have become an actuality.

The following people have been a massive help with my literary endeavours and their support is hugely appreciated: My family, Doug James, Peter Skillen, Murray Denwood, Rob Gate, Fred Moore, Jim Hopkins, Gary Herbert, Craig Strickland, Paul Cartmell, Geoff Thompson, Peter Consterdine and Dawn, Stewart Ferris, Rosalind Hart, all at Summersdale Publishers, Bob Sykes, Moira Spencer, all at Martial Arts Illustrated magazine, Roddie Grant and the team at My Word, Tony Mottram, Martyn Goodfellow, Dan Redmond, Paul Clifton and all at Traditional Karate and Combat Magazines, all those who purchased my previous material, and everyone who so kindly wrote to me to voice their support for my efforts.

Above all I'd like to thank my beautiful wife Helen for all her love, unerring support, and for the happiness brought to me by her and our much-loved sons, David and Rhys.

Warning

The methods described and demonstrated in this book are potentially dangerous and must not be attempted by anyone unless they are under expert supervision. Any persons attempting any of the activities described in this book do so entirely at their own risk. All readers are encouraged to be aware of, and adhere to, all appropriate laws relating to self-defence.

Contents

Introduction

In recent times, more and more martial artists are critically re-evaluating the effectiveness of their chosen art. The need for skills at all ranges of combat is now more widely understood. You could be the best kicker in the world, but if you don't know how to grapple you will be easily defeated if your opponent gets inside kicking range (which isn't that hard to do). Also, just suppose that you're a great wrestler, but have had no exposure to striking. It may take you longer to defeat an opponent (strikes being a quicker way to end fights), you will be very vulnerable to strikes and, most importantly of all, you will not have the ability to 'stun and run', which is vital for effective self-protection.

A chain is only as strong as its weakest link. To be a truly effective fighter, you will need to be conversant with all ranges of combat. This realisation has lead to strikers learning how to grapple, and grapplers learning to strike. However, one question that needs to be asked is, 'why doesn't the art you already practise have those missing skills on its curriculum?' If the original martial arts were designed for use in real combat, then why are there such glaring omissions?

Over the last century, the martial arts have undergone many significant changes. Most important of all has been a fundamental change to the goals of training. The original goal of all the martial arts was the defeat of an opponent in military or civilian combat, but the focus of many systems has now changed. Most practitioners of the martial arts, whether they realise it or not, now train for physical development or sport.

For the practitioner who trains in the martial arts to stay in shape, it does not really matter if all ranges of combat are practised. All that is needed is for the training to be physically taxing enough to improve their level of fitness. Likewise, if the same practitioner has the necessary muscle control, flexibility and physical strength to perform the various physical movements, katas, forms, prearranged techniques etc, it is irrelevant whether they have the skill to actually apply those movements in live combat. In today's martial arts, mastery of physical movement is often all that is required to advance through the grades. Hence, we have the situation where many higher grades, though technically competent, are not actually able to apply what they have learnt in live situations.

The other modern trend in the martial arts is the shift towards sport. In this instance, the goal is the acquisition of trophies and titles through the defeat of practitioners of the same discipline in a rule-bound environment. This evolution has seen those techniques that are not associated with sporting success fall by the wayside. Karate, boxing, taekwondo etc have always favoured striking methods, and that is why their sporting versions have evolved into solely striking affairs. Judo, on the other hand, has always favoured grappling. Judo did originally contain striking techniques. However, the rules of competitive judo prohibit striking, hence you would now find it fairly difficult to find a judo club that teaches striking. The older versions of karate and taekwondo contained throws, joint-locks, strangles etc. Again, many of these techniques are now banned in the modern sporting versions of karate and taekwondo, and therefore very few schools now teach the grappling side of those arts.

Not only do these modern evolutions limit the techniques available to the art's practitioners, they also increase their vulnerabilities. For example, because wrestlers never have to face kicks and punches in a competitive bout, they are never exposed to strikes and are therefore unlikely to be able to deal with them effectively. Conversely, the modern boxer will be highly skilled at dealing with punches, but will be vulnerable to kicks, throws etc.

The original fighting arts were for use in real combat, and therefore they covered all ranges. The karateka of the past covered throwing, grappling, locking etc in their training (see my books, *Karate's Grappling Methods* and *Bunkai-Jutsu: The Practical Application of Karate Kata*). So did boxers, kung-fu stylists and practitioners of what became known as taekwondo. A quick look through the history books, and an examination of the traditional forms, reveals grappling techniques in abundance.

Karate was strongly influenced by many differing styles of Chinese boxing. This included the methods of Shuai Jiao (a form of Chinese wrestling that is said to date back to 2000 BC) and Chin-Na (seizing and joint locking). Karate has also been influenced by the native Okinawan grappling art of Tegumi and, to a lesser degree, the Aiki-Jujitsu systems of the Japanese samurai.

Boxing also used to contain many grappling and throwing techniques. It is believed that modern boxing (and wrestling) evolved from the Greek art of Pankration (meaning 'all powerful'). This art contained strikes, holds, throws, ground fighting and submissions. Greek mythology states that both Hercules and Theseus were skilled in the art of Pankration.

In more recent times, there is an abundance of records that refer to boxers using grappling and throwing techniques. As an example, James Figg – who was the first ever bare-knuckle boxing champion of England – defended his title against Ned Sutton in 1727. It is recorded that Figg winded Sutton by throwing him on his back, and that Figg eventually won the bout by knocking Sutton down and pinning him until he submitted! These techniques are now never seen in the modern sport of boxing. However, they were a part of the original system. Boxing was taught as a self-defence system to society gentlemen. The first gloves were developed so that they could practise the art without picking up bumps and bruises that were not befitting their status. Throwing was also considered to be an important part of the self-defence side of boxing.

Taekwondo is a relatively modern art, the name 'taekwondo' first being used in 1955. However, it is said that its origins go back much further. Taekwondo is based on the warrior art of Tae Kyon, which was formulated by the warriors of the Koguryo kingdom and was then spread to the whole of Korea by the Hwarang (warrior class) of the Silla kingdom. The Korean arts of Subak, Kwonbop and Cireum (a wrestling art based on Chinese and Mongolian systems) are also said to have influenced the development of what became taekwondo. Chinese kempo and in particular Okinawan and Japanese karate have also influenced modern taekwondo. Indeed, many of the original taekwondo forms were based on the karate katas. These 'common forms' mean that taekwondo will also have been influenced by Okinawan and Japanese grappling and throwing techniques. Whilst grappling is not a commonly practised part of the art today, we can see that grappling techniques were a part of the systems upon which the modern art of taekwondo is based.

Although many styles of kung-fu are now practised as striking only systems, wrestling and joint-locking are traditionally regarded as a standard part of all Chinese martial arts. Traditional kung-fu is said to be made up of four sections: striking, kicking, wrestling and joint-locks. We have already discussed how the methods of Chinese wrestling have influenced karate and taekwondo. The Japanese methods of jujitsu (upon which modern judo is based) were also hugely influenced by Chinese grappling methods. As with karate and taekwondo, a study of the traditional forms will often reveal many grappling and throwing techniques.

Not only did the striking arts originally contain grappling and throwing techniques, grappling arts such as wrestling, judo, aikido etc also originally contained striking techniques. It is only in relatively recent times that the martial arts have narrowed their focus. However, this narrowing of focus has had a positive side. Because the vast majority of boxers have now abandoned the grappling side of their art to concentrate solely on punching, they have become exceptional punchers. Judoka are without a doubt the premier throwers of the martial arts community due to the heavy focus they now place on throwing.

The original arts, although much more broad based, were not as sophisticated as their modern counterparts. The modern practitioners of the various arts have taken certain aspects to levels never dreamed of by their predecessors, and this has benefited the martial arts as a whole. However, some aspects of these increased levels of sophistication can bring their own problems, which we will discuss in the following chapter.

It must also be understood that communication was very limited during the times our arts were being developed. Today, it is possible to learn many arts from all over the world. In the past, however, people would only be able to study with practitioners who lived in their local area. For example, the boxers of England would not have been able to study with the jujitsu practitioners of Japan. This is one more reason why the techniques of the older arts are not always as sophisticated as those we have access to today. This lack of sophistication does not mean these techniques are ineffective, far from it. However, it must be said that the 'forgotten' aspects of the older arts are often not as refined as the techniques of those arts now dedicated to particular skills (as you would expect).

If effective fighting skills are your aim, then you need to include all ranges of combat in your training. There are essentially two ways to ensure that your training is broad based. The first is to study a variety of arts ('cross-training' as it is often called). For example, you may study boxing for your punches, taekwondo for your kicking, and judo for your grappling. This is obviously a great way to train because you are effectively learning the strongest aspects of the various arts. The downside is that you may become a 'jack of all trades and a master of none'. And unless you get sufficient guidance from experienced cross-trainers, the various methods can become disjointed with none of the systems being practised gelling together.

The second way to ensure your training is broad based is to study the older version of your current art. The advantage of this approach is that you will be learning a single complete and coherent system. The negative side is that the methods of the older version of your art will often not be as sophisticated or refined as those of the dedicated grappling arts (and it can also be hard finding an instructor who teaches the older version of the system). If you're a boxer, you could learn the throws that were once a fundamental part of boxing. If you're a karate, taekwondo or kung-fu practitioner, you could examine the grappling techniques that are recorded within your forms. You should understand that studying the throwing techniques of the striking arts will in no way make you the equal of a judoka or wrestler when it comes to throws. However, a study of the 'forgotten' throws will give you the fundamental throwing skills that may be needed for self-protection. It's really a matter of what you as an individual require from your training.

My personal approach has been to fully study my chosen art (karate), and to examine the methods of dedicated grappling arts to increase my understanding of the techniques already present in my base system. However, as I said, it's really a matter of what works best for you. Some of my training partners and students also study judo, which has not only enhanced their application of the basic throwing techniques found within the traditional forms, but it has also furthered their knowledge and understanding of throwing techniques in general.

There are many different aspects to grappling. In this book we will be concentrating on the throws and takedowns that were once a common part of the striking arts. Differing arts may have emphasised certain throws over others, or have performed them in slightly differing ways to those shown here. However, the throws shown in this book are common to many arts (grappling and striking) and, in my opinion, are some of the most effective throws for use in self-defence. Exploring all the throws originally found in what are now called the 'striking systems' would be a huge task. It is hoped that the throws covered in this book will help you to further explore the specific throws found within your own system. You may not perform the throws covered in exactly the same way as demonstrated, but the fundamental concepts are common to all systems. What works, works!

The purpose of this book is to help practitioners of the striking arts to reintroduce the throwing methods that were once part of their system. This will then allow you to practise your art as its founders originally intended. These throws can obviously also be found in the grappling systems and we will make reference to these arts where appropriate.

Chapter 1

The use of throws in the striking arts

To begin this chapter, I should probably define what I mean by 'striking arts' and 'grappling arts'. As we discussed in the introduction, originally all the arts contained both grappling and striking methods (as both are required for effective fighting). However, it is fair to say that the arts rarely placed an equal emphasis on each method. The emphasis placed upon each aspect would depend upon the environment and culture in which the system was to be used.

Karate, for example, has always placed a much heavier emphasis on striking. This is because karate is a civil system (formulated by unarmed civilians) and striking is the most effective tool for use in that environment. The original practitioners of karate practised grappling techniques, but striking was always given priority. So it would be fair to class karate as a 'striking art' even though grappling is also a part of the original system.

Judo, on the other hand, has always placed a heavy emphasis on grappling. This is because judo is based on the battlefield art of jujitsu. On the battlefield, the warriors would be armed and they would be wearing armour. This meant that weapons would always be used as the first option. If a warrior, who had lost their sword or spear, got close enough to fight hands on, striking with the bare hands would be ineffective due to their opponent's armour. It would therefore make much more sense to grapple and control an opponent so that they could be finished off with a close range weapon such as a knife. Striking would have been practised, but a samurai would always use weapons first, grappling second and strikes last. Hence, grappling would be given priority during unarmed training and therefore judo and jujitsu are classed as 'grappling systems', even though both systems also contain striking techniques.

So when I talk about 'striking arts', I mean arts where the emphasis is placed upon striking, but basic grappling skills are also practised. Of course, in many cases the 'striking arts' have now evolved into 'striking only' systems, but it should be remembered that they were not originally practised that way.

In modern-day civilian self-protection, the emphasis should most definitely be placed upon striking. This is because is takes time to grapple an opponent into submission, their grip will prevent you from escaping, and you will be very vulnerable to the strikes of your opponent's accomplices.

In a 'square go', where two fighters square off, begin fighting on an agreed signal, and where no one else is going to get involved (such as in a martial arts tournament) it is a safe assumption that the better grappler will win. This has led many martial artists to wrongly conclude that grappling is the best way to defend yourself – it isn't!

Live fights are rarely one-on-one for any length of time. To tie up your hands by grabbing a single opponent at the onset of an attack is not at all wise. Being capable of delivering strong strikes – preferably pre-emptively during the dialogue stages of the altercation – is the key skill required for effective self-protection (see Geoff Thompson's book, *The Fence*).

If your strike is strong enough, you will be able to escape whilst the opponent is stunned. If your assailant manages to secure a grip on you prior to the delivery of a strike, or if your strike did not have the desired effect and the opponent closed the distance, then you need to know how to grapple.

Being at close-range does not mean it is time to stop striking, just the opposite in fact. Continue to strike the opponent until they are incapacitated or you have the opportunity to flee. Striking should always remain the priority. However, should one of your strikes weaken or unbalance the opponent – but not in a way that allows you to flee – you may wish to exploit that opportunity and throw the opponent to the floor. If you can manage to throw the opponent cleanly you will have a large advantage and a great opportunity to run away.

Throws are techniques of opportunity. You take them if the opportunity should present itself, but you should not be looking for throws in the first instance. Throughout this book, the majority of the throws demonstrated are preceded by a strike. You must understand that the aim of the strike is to finish off the opponent. The fact that it may set up a throw is incidental, not intentional. To go looking for throws in the first instance is foolhardy (unless you are an exceptional thrower, and as a practitioner of a striking system that is very unlikely). The reason why you should not use throws as your main artillery is that people with even just average strength will be able to effectively resist your attempt to throw them. Your chances of success will be markedly increased, however, if the opponent is still reeling from the effects of a strong blow. Always remember to give strikes the priority and only attempt to apply a throw if the effect of one of your blows creates the ideal opportunity.

A strong strike will take away the opponent's presence of mind. If they are aware that they are being thrown there is a good chance that they will panic, secure a firm grip upon you and then try to drag you to the floor with them. In the vast majority of cases, you do not want to go to the floor with your opponent. That said, sometimes you don't have a choice! Later on in this book we'll look at what to do if your opponent manages to take you to the floor with them. However, for now it is important to understand that the chances of you going to the floor will be reduced if the opponent is dazed and confused. In fact, you'd be well advised not to attempt a throw unless the opponent is in that condition.

If you do manage to successfully throw your opponent, your safety is in no way guaranteed despite your advantageous position. As soon as your opponent hits the floor you should instantly escape or follow up. If you simply stand back and admire your work, your opponent will be given the opportunity to get back up and continue their assault.

It is important to keep everything as simple as possible. In a real situation, you will be throwing the opponent after they have been struck, and the opponent is very unlikely to be a skilled grappler. In a wrestling or judo competition, the participants will not have been disoriented by strikes and they will be highly skilled at avoiding being thrown. This means that their skill level will need to be very high if they are going to be able to throw their opponent. They will need to be able to confuse and mislead the opponent, use feints, execute counter-throws etc. None of which is really relevant to a self-defence situation where the opponent is very unlikely to respond to feints etc.

In modern martial arts, many practitioners mistake 'advanced' for 'effective' and wrongly assume that simple techniques are inferior to their advanced counterparts. However, it is true that simple and direct techniques are less likely to work when facing someone of the same discipline in a rule-bound environment (where many of the simplest techniques will be banned anyway). Competitors and coaches invariably develop more complex and sophisticated methods in order to catch their opponents off-guard. These complex techniques, whilst ideal for use by highly trained athletes in a rule-bound environment, can be ineffective when used by less gifted people outside that environment. Very few people have the necessary physical skills to make many of the more elaborate methods work. The more basic a technique is, the more likely it is to work in a self-defence situation. The fact that you should have struck the opponent prior to attempting a throw further negates the need for more elaborate methods.

If you want to have the skills needed to outwrestle a trained grappler, or if you wish to take your grappling skills to a high level, then you obviously need to study a dedicated grappling art. If, however, you want to have a knowledge of simple throws for use in self-defence, that can be used to back up your striking, then you'll probably find everything you need in the older version of your art.

If you practise an art that has forms/katas/hyungs on its curriculum, there is a strong chance you already practise the basic mechanics of throwing without even realising it. The forms of most martial arts (being a record of the older version of the art) tend to contain methods for use at all ranges, including grappling and throwing. The problem is that they are rarely recognised as such because they are mistaken for strikes and blocks. This is again due to the narrowing focus of the 'striking arts' so that every movement of the form is either interpreted as a strike or a defensive movement against a strike... even when such interpretations are obviously woefully inadequate!

At the end of this book there is a section that shows how some of the throws covered in this book are recorded within the forms. You may not practise the exact same forms as those shown, or you may perform them in different ways, but it is hoped that the examples will act as food for thought and help you to recognise throws in your own forms.

Before we go on to have a look at the throws themselves, we will spend the next chapter looking at the theories behind throwing and the training methods that will give you the skills to put those theories into practise.

Chapter 2

Theory and practise

We will begin this chapter by looking at some of the fundamentals of throwing. Without a sound working knowledge of these basic principles it will be difficult to execute the throws discussed in the following chapters. The first thing we shall look at is the importance of grip.

When attempting to throw the opponent, you must have sufficient control over their movement. This control is achieved by seizing the opponent in the correct way. Whilst the exact grip employed is dependant upon the technique being applied, there are some fundamentals that apply to all grips.

Essentially there are two types of grip: those that rely upon the opponent's clothing and those that do not. If we look at the jacketed grappling systems, such as judo or sombo (a Russian fighting system that gets its name from the Russian for 'self-defence without weapons'), it is fairly common for the clothing to be used to secure a grip. In wrestling, on the other hand, no jacket is worn so the grips have to be secured upon the opponent's anatomy. Within the forms of karate, taekwondo etc, there are throws that use clothing and throws that do not. The boxers of old fought bare-chested. Hence, they would not use clothing for the throwing techniques they used in the ring (although the occasional gripping of the trousers to effect a throw may have occurred until it was banned in 1743). However, boxing was also originally practised as a self-defence system, so some techniques that did seize the clothing of the torso may also have been practised.

I prefer to emphasise gripping the anatomy as opposed to clothing, because the latter cannot always be relied upon. If the opponent was wearing a shirt or T-shirt, it is unlikely to provide a secure grip as it will rip fairly easily. If the opponent was wearing a thick jacket, or similar item of clothing, then it could definitely be used to your advantage. However, in this book we will concentrate on gripping the opponent's body, because that option is always available.

The grips required for specific techniques will be covered in the relevant chapter. For now, we will cover the more general grips needed to control the opponent whilst fighting at grappling range. When fighting at close-range your grip on the opponent serves two functions. Firstly, your grip should control the opponent's movements. This includes controlling the opponent's limbs so that they can't strike you, and controlling their movement so that you can create opportunities for your own techniques. The second function of grips is to inform you of your opponent's motion and intentions so that you can take appropriate action. It is vital that you are sensitive to your opponent's movements and that you do not just rely upon raw strength when fighting at close-range. We will discuss some drills that you can use to help develop this sensitivity later on in this chapter.

There are essentially four key places to seize the opponent for general control: the back of the neck, the back (just below the shoulder blade), the top of the forearm and the back of the upper arm. The first two (neck and back) are used to control and inform you of the opponent's body motion. The second two (forearm and back of upper arm) are used to control and monitor the opponent's arm.

Examples of grips in use

Figure 1:
Back of neck and
forearm grip

▼

Figure 2:
Upper arm and
back grip

▼

Figure 3:
Back of neck and
upper arm grip

▼

If you look at the pictures of the grips in use, you will notice how the head is consistently positioned close to the opponent on the side where the arm is controlled. This defensive position makes it difficult for your opponent to deliver punches to your head. However, your view of the opponent is greatly reduced whilst in this position (as is often the case at close-range). This emphasises the importance of using your grip to inform you of your opponent's movements.

Practitioners of grappling arts are very sensitive to the movement of their opponents. Nowadays, practitioners of striking arts tend not to be. This is because seizing the opponent is generally prohibited by modern rules and hence the referee will stop the bout and restart it at 'striking range'. Even many of those not involved in sporting martial arts tend to abide by this unwritten rule (probably because they wish to stay at a distance where they know what they are doing). However, if effective fighting skills are your aim, then it is vital that you get plenty of practise at fighting from a clinch.

It should also be remembered that striking is always the preferred option, even within grappling range. Therefore, you will also need to practise delivering and defending against strikes from a clinch (more on that later).

Another fundamental of throwing is balance. There are two sides to balance. Firstly, maintaining your own balance, and secondly, breaking your opponent's balance. The laws of physics state that an object will fall when its centre of gravity is moved outside its base area. In the human body, the centre of gravity is located a few inches below the navel in the centre of the body. This point is often referred to as the 'hara' or 'tanden'. Once this point is outside the area covered by the feet, the body will fall. If you stand with your feet together and start to lean forwards, you will notice that once the hara gets beyond the toes you will topple forward. This position is often called 'the point of no return'. To prevent yourself from falling you are very likely to take a step forwards. This will increase the area covered by your feet so that the centre of gravity is once again inside the base area. Hence you don't fall. We can therefore see that to keep your balance you must keep the hara inside the base area covered by your feet. Conversely, to break the opponent's balance, you need to move their hara outside the area covered by their feet.

We will look at maintaining our own balance first. There are two key things we must do to keep the hara inside our base area. Firstly, we must keep the hara low. Secondly, we must have as large a base area as possible. Take a look at the triangles in Figure Four. (**Figure 4**)

The sloping sides of both triangles are the same length, and are meant to represent the legs. The centre of gravity is located at the top of these triangles,

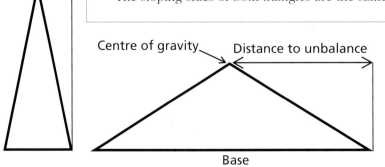

Centre of gravity

Distance to unbalance

Base

Figure 4

in the same way that a human's centre of gravity is found at the top of the legs. It should be obvious from looking at the triangles that the one on the left would be the easiest to tip over. This is because the centre of gravity is higher and the base area is smaller. This means that the centre of gravity does not have to move very far before it is outside the base area. And when it does, the triangle will fall. The triangle on the left has a lower centre of gravity and a much wider base. The centre of gravity now has much further to go before it would be outside the base area.

It should now be apparent that the best way to ensure you are stable is to keep your hips low and your feet far apart. Look at the grips shown in Figures One, Two and Three. Notice how the hips are low and the feet are away from one another. This is of course quite different from the stances used outside grappling range where the stances are generally much higher. This is because a lower stance, whilst very stable, is a lot less mobile. It is simply a matter of distributing your weight as required at any particular moment in time. In order to keep your balance during grappling, the stance should be deep and wide.

I'd better more clearly define what I mean by 'stance'. It is vitally important that you keep moving when fighting. The word 'stance' has connotations of something fixed and immovable, but it must be understood that you should be constantly changing your stance relative to the situation. When grappling, you should be constantly moving your feet relative to the opponent's motion and the techniques you are applying at that point. As you move around, you should be in a stance that keeps your hips low, your feet apart and your centre of gravity inside the area covered by your feet. The stance is not fixed, but pliable, as all stances should be.

We'll now move on to breaking the opponent's balance. As already mentioned, the key to breaking the opponent's balance is to move their hara outside their base area. It should now be apparent from the discussion on maintaining your own balance that the two keys to achieving this are to raise the opponent's hara and reduce the base area covered by their feet. When you go through the chapters on the actual throws, notice how the techniques destroy the opponent's base, raise the hara and often both. As we mentioned in the previous chapter, the best way to set an opponent up for a throw is to deliver a hard strike. You can of course further break the opponent's balance by pulling or pushing them.

The art of breaking the opponent's balance by pulling or pushing is called 'Kuzushi' in Japanese. It is commonly taught that there are eight directions in which to break the opponent's balance. These are to the rear, to the front, to the left, to the right and the diagonals in-between (eg rear and to the left). This does not mean that you can use all eight at any one time. The direction of the push or pull is dependent upon the opponent's posture. The key to unbalancing the opponent is to move the hara outside the base area. This is best achieved by pushing or pulling the opponent at a ninety-degree angle to the line of their feet. This is the key principle upon which the techniques of unbalancing rest. It is at this angle that the opponent's base is at its narrowest. The hara will not have to move very far before it is outside the base area and hence the opponent will lose their balance. Pushing or pulling at an angle between the ideal of ninety degrees and forty-five degrees to the line of the feet is still likely to unbalance the opponent. However, the opponent will have a very easy time resisting you if your push is at an angle of less than forty-five degrees. Therefore, of the eight possible directions, at any instant the opponent will be:

- very vulnerable to two (those at ninety-degrees to the line of the feet);
- relatively vulnerable to four (those at forty-five degrees to the line of the feet);
- not vulnerable to the remaining two (those in line with the feet).

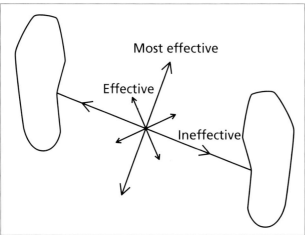

Figure 5: Directions of unbalancing

If you were to stand with your feet in a straight line, and you were pushed or pulled in exactly the same direction as that line, you would be relatively stable. If, however, you were pushed at a ninety-degree angle to the line of your feet, you will be extremely easy to unbalance. Regardless of where your opponent has placed their feet, they are always in a straight line when considered from the correct angle. If you pull or push at ninety-degrees to this line then the opponent will become unbalanced. If the opponent has a good sense of balance, they will quickly move one of their feet so that you are no longer pushing or pulling at the correct angle. The fact that they are regaining their balance means that they are unable to do anything else at that moment in time. This makes it an ideal time to launch a further attack (a strike, a throw, unbalance them again etc).

So far in this chapter we have discussed the fundamental theories associated with grips, stance and balance. The next thing to cover is putting the theories into practise. If you've read any of my previous books, you will already be familiar with some of the following drills.

Safety in practise

Before we go on to describe the various practise drills, we will discuss some key safety considerations. Suitable mats must be used during throwing practise. The mats must be thick enough to absorb impact and should not easily move apart. The mats we use in my own dojo were once used in military training. They absorb impact well, have edges that attach to the neighbouring mat and never move apart no matter how energetic the practise (they are so heavy it even takes two people to lift a single section!). You should also ensure that the matted area is large enough and keep all practise towards the centre of the mat. If you do not, there is a possibility that your partner could land on an un-matted area.

It is also very important that you look after your partner's safety, and that they look after yours. Execute all techniques with care and try to apply them in a way that ensures your partner can land safely (eg don't drop them on their head or neck!). In live practise, any technique that you find difficult to control should be omitted until you have acquired sufficient skill to execute it safely. You must practise landing safely. Ensure that your chin is tucked in towards your chest so that your head does not hit the floor. You should also ensure that you do not land directly on your back, elbows, base of your spine, nape of your neck etc.

To begin with, it is best to practise all techniques slowly. This will ensure correct form is developed whilst allowing the person being thrown to practise landing safely. In some of the drills we will discuss, striking is allowed. For those drills you must make sure you are wearing all the required protective equipment, eg gloves (ideally ones that still allow grabbing), gum-shield, box, chest-guard, head-guard etc. All training should also be closely supervised. You must only practise the techniques and drills described in this book whilst under competent supervision. It is also vital that you get yourself checked out by a doctor before engaging in this type of training.

The drills

You must practise your throwing techniques against an opponent who does not wish to be thrown, because that is what you will be facing in reality. This may seem like an obvious statement to make; however there are many that believe gentle practise with a compliant partner is all that is required. Trying to throw someone who does not want to be thrown is not at all easy. That is why many people prefer to take the easy route and omit non-compliant practise from their training. It can also be a bit of a blow to the ego to discover that techniques – which looked and felt great when practised with a compliant partner – either don't work or are now very rough around the edges. However, if real and effective skills are your aim, you have to put your ego aside and engage in non-compliant training. When you manage to throw an opponent, despite their best efforts to stay upright, it gives you a huge confidence boost. You now know you can make your techniques work against an uncooperative opponent, because you've done just that!

An analogy I often like to use is that of a carpenter and his tools. A carpenter will need a good set of tools if he is to produce good quality work. Likewise, a martial artist will need good techniques if they are to be able to fight effectively. However, just having a good set of tools will not guarantee the carpenter's work will be of a high quality. It is the skill of the carpenter to use those tools that determines the quality of the end result. Similarly, it is not a martial artist's techniques that determines how good a fighter they are, but how well they can apply those techniques. A carpenter has to get his tools out of the box and practise using them on wood if he is to learn his trade. A martial artist has to use their techniques in live practise if they are to learn theirs!

The learning stage

You must be sure to pay great attention to detail when first learning the techniques described in this book. It is vital that you develop good form if the techniques are going to work for you. Practise the techniques slowly with a partner who offers no resistance. Then, as your skills improve, practise the techniques a little faster with a little more free movement. Your partner should also start to offer a little resistance, not so much resistance that you are unable to practise the technique, but enough that ensures your technique is correct. Once the actual execution of the throw is thoroughly understood, you must move on from compliant practise.

Grips and unbalancing

This drill will develop your ability to apply and defend against grips, in addition to teaching you how to unbalance the opponent whilst maintaining your own balance. You and a partner take hold of one another and then attempt to push or pull each other off balance. You should ensure that your stance is stable and that you use the most appropriate grip at that particular time. Try to move your partner at ninety degrees to the line of their feet (as discussed earlier). Also try to use your sense of touch and don't just rely on your vision. For example, if your head is so close to your partner that you can't see their feet (as it often is), you may simply decide to push in any direction. If you feel that the opponent is very stable in the direction of the push, then you are probably pushing along the line of the feet, or close to it. You should then quickly pull or push your partner at ninety degrees to the direction of the initial push which, with a bit of luck, should unbalance them.

As your partner endeavours to unbalance you, you should move your feet so that your balance is maintained. We discussed the theory of keeping your balance earlier in this chapter. The best way to ensure that you understand this theory is to put it into practise! And that is exactly what this drill will do.

Grips and striking

We have already covered the importance of being able to deliver strikes at close range. This drill will help you to develop those skills. It starts with both participants securing a grip on one another. One is given the role of striker, whilst the other is given the role of defender. As is suggested by the title, the striker must try to free their limbs and strike their partner. The defender's job is to tie up the striker's limbs so that they cannot strike effectively. After an agreed period of time, the participants should change roles.

Throws only

Both participants take hold of each other and endeavour to throw each other to the ground. If one participant is upright whilst the other is on the ground, then the one who is upright is declared the winner. If both participants should fall to the floor, then the bout is stopped and restarted with both people back on their feet. An interesting variation on this drill is to make one participant the 'thrower' whilst the other simply tries to stay on their feet. After the allotted time has passed, the participants should change roles.

Throwing and striking

As 'throws only,' except the use of strikes is now permitted. It should be remembered that striking is always the preferred option in a real situation. Hence, striking should also be the preferred option in training. If your strikes create the opportunity for a throw, then take it, but don't go looking for throws in the first instance. If heavy contact is to be used, then the winner is the one who manages to take the other off their feet, either through being knocked down by the strikes, or through the application of a throw. If control is to be applied, a ruling on what strikes will be classed as winning blows should be made, eg 'three head punches in a three-second period'. The person supervising the fight should then declare the winner when that requirement is met or a successful throw is executed.

Whoops!

Not every technique works exactly as we would like it to, and we need to know what to do should everything go wrong! If we should attempt a throw and end up on the floor with our opponent, or worse still end up on the floor alone, we need to ensure that we practise taking the correct action. We will discuss the exact nature of what to do in Chapter 14, but we'll briefly cover the associated drill now because it is an important part of throwing as a whole.

Both participants take up a position on the floor. One person tries to stand back up, whilst the other attempts to keep them on the floor. If the person trying to regain their feet should do so, then they should quickly lie back down and continue as before until the designated time has passed. Both participants will then change roles.

The other scenario is that the opponent is on their feet whilst you are on the floor. The key thing is to keep your feet towards your opponent as you make the room to get up safely (more in Chapter 14). To practise this, one person will lie down on the floor. The person standing up then attempts to tap their partner on the torso, arms or head (the legs don't count). If they can tap their partner, using either their hands or feet, then they are the winner. The person on the floor has to get to a vertical position without being tapped in order to win.

Combined drills

It is possible to combine any of the drills described in this section. For example, you could practise 'grips and unbalancing', and should either or both of you fall over, you could go straight into the 'whoops!' drill. You could also combine the 'grips and striking' drill with the 'throws only' drills so that one person is striking, whilst the other is trying not to get hit and throw the other to the ground. The possibilities are endless and I'm sure that you will be able to think up many very productive drills of your own. The key thing is to ensure that you practise the techniques described in this book in a realistic fashion because that is the only way to develop real skill.

In this chapter, we have covered the basic theories associated with throws, and the drills that will ensure that we have the skills to put those theories into practise. We'll now move on to look at the actual throws that were once a common part of the striking arts.

Chapter 3

Sweeps

Sweeps are arguably the most basic of all throws, and there are many different ways to apply them. It is possible to apply sweeps before you and the opponent have latched onto one another, which is how they are most commonly used in the modern day versions of the striking arts. Trap the opponent's lead arm and deliver an open-handed strike to their jaw (**Figure 1**). The force of the blow will weaken and distract the opponent in addition to taking the weight off their lead leg. Sweep the opponent's lead foot as you transfer your body weight onto your back foot. Contact should be made with the sole of your foot. Making contact with the inside edge is both painful to the sweeper and less effective. It is important to use your hips and move the opponent's leg across, and away from them, in order to unbalance the opponent as much as possible (**Figure 2**). However, if the opponent does manage to stay upright, you should promptly strike again whilst they are still off balance. This second blow may very well knock the opponent to the ground and finish what the sweep started.

There are many differing ways in which the opponent can be swept. One way in which you can use the movement of the arms to set up the sweep is as follows. The opponent has

Figure 1

Figure 2

Figure 3

Figure 4

Figure 5

Figure 6

seized your clothing. Deliver a front kick to the shin of the opponent's lead leg (**Figure 3**). Quickly move your hands to the opponent's elbows. Push the opponent's elbows in a circular fashion so that they are forced to lean towards the leg you have just kicked (**Figure 4**). Keep pushing on the opponent's elbows as you sweep out their lead leg (**Figure 5**). This type of sweep is found in the taekwondo form of Chul Ghi and the karate kata Naihanchi (upon which the Korean version is based).

If you have scooped up your opponent's kick, or reached down and lifted the opponent's lead leg off the floor, you could throw the opponent by lifting them slightly and then sweeping their supporting leg off the floor (**Figure 6**). There are many ways of sweeping the opponent and you are encouraged to experiment with the use of sweeps in your training.

Chapter 4

The hip throw

In this chapter we will look at the basic hip throw (Ogoshi). As its name suggests, the hip throw involves taking the opponent over your hip and onto the floor. The hip throw is often one of the first throws taught throughout the martial arts. The reason for this is that the hip throw is relatively simple to learn, and the basic movement is also used in other throwing techniques.

The big drawback with the hip throw, and others like it, is that it involves turning your back on the opponent. Should the throw fail, the opponent will be left in a dominant position. In order to increase the chances of the throw being successful, it is vital to ensure the opponent is weakened and that their balance has been broken. It is also important to apply the throw as vigorously as possible. If the opponent should manage to drop their weight and successfully defend against the throw, you should immediately abandon the throw, reverse your footwork and quickly return to a position where you are facing the opponent.

From a clinch, strike the opponent's jaw with your head (**Figure 1**). Feed your right arm around the opponent's back, as your right foot moves towards your opponent's right foot. You should turn so that your legs are bent and your hips are lower than your opponent's. On the completion of the turn, both of your feet should be inside the opponent's feet, and pointing in the same direction. It is also important to ensure that there is no gap between the opponent's body and your own. The left arm should keep a tight grip on the opponent's right triceps and

Figure 1

Figure 2

Figure 3

Figure 4

pull the opponent in the direction of the turn. Both of your arms should pull the opponent forwards so that they are tilted in that direction (**Figure 2**). Straighten your knees and lean your upper-body forward so that your hips push through the opponent's thighs. Simultaneously continue to pull the opponent forwards so that their feet are raised off the floor and the opponent is lifted onto your hips (**Figure 3**). Continue the rotation of the arms to take the opponent over the back of your hips to complete the throw (**Figure 4**).

The hip throw is found towards the end of the karate and taekwondo form Pinan/Heian/Pyung Ann 3. This movement is shown in the appendix at the end of this book.

Chapter 5

The cross-buttocks throw

The cross-buttocks throw is a technique found in most styles. However, the term 'cross-buttocks' is most commonly used in the various forms of wrestling. It was also a much-used technique in boxing (the original bare-knuckle variety) until the introduction of modern rules resulted in the demise of the grappling side of the art. The first set of rules were introduced to boxing in 1743 by Jack Broughton – champion for two decades – after one of his opponents (George Stevenson) died after their bout. Among other things, Broughton's rules outlawed the hitting and kicking of a man when he was down, and the seizing of the opponent below the waist. However, it was still perfectly legitimate to seize the opponent above the waist in order to secure them for a blow, or to throw them. One possible match tactic (not to be confused with the strategy employed when boxing was being used for self-defence) was to throw the opponent in such a way that the thrower would land on top of the recipient. This was done in the hope of injuring them so that they would not be able to continue in the allotted time. The cross-buttocks throw was a major part of a boxer's arsenal at that time.

Jack Broughton was the inventor of the first pair of boxing gloves, or 'mufflers' as they were called. These gloves were not worn in actual bouts, but they were worn in training. It was hoped that the use of mufflers would make boxing more accessible to society gentlemen. Facial injuries were not befitting their social status! In February 1747, Jack Broughton placed an advertisement in *The Daily Advertiser*, which read '*Mr Broughton proposes to open an academy at his house in the Haymarket, for the instruction of those who are willing to be initiated in the mystery of boxing, where the whole theory and practise of that truly British art, with all the various stops, blows, cross-buttocks etc will be fully taught and explained; and that persons of quality and distinction may not be debarred from entering into a course of those lectures, they will be given the utmost tenderness and regard to the delicacy of their frame and constitution of the pupil; for which reason mufflers are provided, that will effectively secure them from the inconvenience of black eyes, broken jaws, and bloody noses.'* From the preceding advert, we can see that Broughton lists the cross-buttocks throw as a key part of boxing skills.

The cross-buttocks throw is found in most styles of wrestling, and is popular in Cumberland and Westmoreland wrestling. As a native of that district – 'Cumberland' being the old name for what is now 'Cumbria' – there is a brewery not far from my home that makes a beer called 'Cross-Buttocks'. The beer is named after one of the main throws of our local fighting art, and the label on the bottle features a picture of a wrestler executing the throw.

The cross-buttocks throw is also found within judo and jujitsu, although it tends to be referred to as 'Koshiguruma' (hip wheel). However, the judo and jujitsu version of the throw is performed in a slightly different way (the hips are in line rather than taken past).

The cross-buttocks throw is also very common within taekwondo and karate forms. However, it is often mistaken as a 'turning lower-block' or similar, and as a result the cross-buttocks throw is now rarely practised in taekwondo and karate circles, despite the number of times it appears in the forms. We will show examples of where throws appear in the katas / forms in the appendix.

The cross-buttocks throw is very effective and that is why it is so common throughout the martial arts. There are a few variations of this technique depending upon how the opponent has been seized and the specifics of the style being practised. My favourite is when the opponent's head has been seized. I feel this version gives greater control over the opponent. You also remain in a strong position should the throw fail. Also, should you be taken to the floor with the opponent, you will automatically land in the scarf-hold (see my book *Karate's Grappling Methods* for further details) which will give you the advantage in any ensuing floor fight. However, it is important to be well versed in all three of the variations shown here so that we can effectively throw the opponent regardless of the grip used.

Figure 1

Figure 2

Figure 3

Figure 4

The first variation we will look at is where the head is seized (this technique is found in Pinan/Heian/Pyung Ann 3 and is often mislabelled as a 'forearm block' performed with both fists on the hip). From the clinch shown, secure the back of the opponent's head and push your body forwards in order to head-butt the opponent. On the head-butt, you should ensure that you hit the opponent below their eyebrows, with the area above your eyebrows (**Figure 1**). Keep a tight hold of the opponent's triceps as you turn your body and feed your right arm around the back of the opponent's neck. Pull on the opponent's arm and pull their head in towards your body so that you secure a strong headlock. As you apply the headlock, bring your rear foot towards the opponent (**Figure 2**). Step forwards with your right foot as you push your hips backward so that the left side of your hip is touching the opponent's body. Pull the opponent in the direction of the step so that their upper-body is bent over your hip and their feet are lifted off the ground (**Figure 3**). It is vital that you push your hips far enough back so that they block the path of

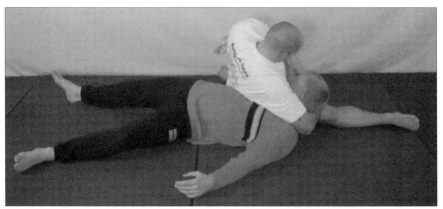

Figure 5

Figure 6

Figure 7

the opponent's legs. Continue to pull with the arms and push with the legs so that the opponent is taken over the back of your hips and onto the floor (**Figure 4**). As mentioned earlier, if the opponent should manage to take you over with them, you will automatically land in the scarf-hold. The nature of the throw also means that you will land directly on top of the opponent (**Figure 5**). Landing on your opponent's ribcage (although never a preferred strategy) can often take away their ability to breathe, and hence their desire to continue the fight. As previously mentioned, landing on the opponent in this way was a technique used in the days of bare-knuckle boxing.

The second variation of this throw is to feed your right arm around the opponent's back, as opposed to encircling their neck. Move your right foot towards the opponent's right foot, and turn so that your foot is pointing away from the opponent. At the same time bring your left foot towards the opponent and feed your right arm under the opponent's armpit and onto their back (**Figure 6**). Step forward with your right foot to position the hips. Pull the opponent as before so that they are taken across the

Figure 8

Figure 9

small of your back and onto the floor. Again, it is important to ensure that hips are pushed past the opponent (**Figure 7**).

The third variation is to feed your free arm under the armpit of the opponent's seized arm. This version is found in a number of karate and taekwondo forms (eg Pinan/Heian/Pyung Ann 5, Chinto/ Gankaku etc) but is often mistaken for a turning block or hammer-fist strike. An elbow strike is delivered to the opponent's jaw (**Figure 8**). The arm is then fed under the opponent's armpit as the back foot is brought towards the opponent. Be sure to keep a tight grip on the opponent's arm and keep it close to you (**Figure 9**). Position the hips as before in order to take the opponent over the back of your hips and onto the floor (**Figure 10**).

Figure 10

Chapter 6

The shoulder throw

There are a number of differing versions of this throw, but the one we will look at here is common to most fighting styles and it does not rely upon the opponent's clothing in order to be effective.

In Cumberland wrestling – and indeed many other forms of western wrestling – this throw is referred to as 'The Flying Mare'. In the Japanese systems (judo, jujitsu etc) it is referred to as 'Seoinage'. The version shown here is specifically called 'Ippon-Seoinage' (one arm shoulder throw). The same throw also appears in a number of kung-fu, karate and taekwondo forms. A notable example is found in the form Pinan/Heian Godan (Pyung Ann 5) where the shoulder throw is followed up with ground fighting control and a cross strangle (this strangle is often mislabelled as a 'lower cross-block').

Figure 1

Deliver an arching palm-heel strike to the opponent's jaw (**Figure 1**). Keep a tight grip on the opponent's arm as you bring your striking arm back and feed it under their armpit (**Figure 2**). Turn your body and bring your feet close together.

Figure 2

Your centre of gravity should be lower than the opponent's and your legs should be bent. Your body should be touching the opponent. It is very important that you pull the opponent's arm down towards your hip at this point. If you do not, the

Figure 3

Figure 4

Figure 5

opponent's arm will be across your neck and this will not only make the throw hard to apply, it will also leave you very vulnerable to being choked or strangled (**Figure 3**). Straighten your legs, pull with the arms and push backward with your hips in order to lift the opponent's feet off the floor (**Figure 4**). Continue the motion in order to throw the opponent to the ground (**Figure 5**).

Chapter 7

The neck throw

This throw can be one of the simplest to apply. The neck throw can be used as an effective follow-up to any striking technique delivered from the outside of the opponent (opponent's entire body to one side). Palm the opponent's lead arm downward as you shift forwards and deliver a right cross to the opponent's jaw (**Figure 1**). Continue to extend the arm, taking it around the opponent's neck whilst stepping past their lead leg with your right foot. As you do so, place your left hand onto the small of the opponent's back (**Figure 2**). Turn your body whilst pushing the opponent in the same direction. The position of your lead leg, and your other hand, will prevent the opponent from stepping back to regain their balance (**Figure 3**).

It is also possible to apply the neck throw by taking the opponent over the back of your hips. This technique places a great deal of pressure upon the opponent's neck and spine, and can cause the opponent to land directly on their head. This version of the neck throw is extremely dangerous and should never be used in live grappling practise. With regards to self-defence, this throw would be wholly unsuitable for anything but life or death situations and is shown here purely for information purposes. Naturally,

Figure 1

Figure 2

Figure 3

Figure 4

Figure 5

such techniques are now also banned from competitive grappling. Following the delivery of the initial right cross, take a big step forwards with your right foot as your right arm goes across the opponent's neck. Bring your left foot up and position your hips so that they are in line with your opponent's hips. Both of your legs should be slightly bent at this point (**Figure 4**). Pull the opponent backwards so that their balance is broken. Your legs should then be straightened in order to take the opponent over the back of your hips (**Figure 5**). If the motion were continued, my partner would land on the back of his head. Hence the conclusion of the throw is not shown (nor should it be practised!).

The neck throw is one of the throws show in Gichin Funakoshi's 1925 book *Rentan Goshin Karate Jutsu* where it appears under the label of 'Kubiwa' (encircle the neck). Gichin Funakoshi was the founder of Shotokan Karate.

Before closing this chapter, I'd like to digress slightly and quickly talk about the right cross used at the start of this technique. Throughout this book, we have been looking at the older versions of the fighting systems covered, and hence I feel it is important we use the appropriate terminology. In the boxing of the past, there was a difference between a 'right cross' and a 'straight right'. Today, both terms are used to describe a straight punch delivered with the right hand whilst the left foot is forward. However, the term 'cross' originally referred to a punch that crossed over the opponent's arm and had a slight hooking action to it. The punch at the start of this technique did just that, and hence the correct term is 'right cross'. To refer to the technique as a 'straight right' would be incorrect when discussing the older style of boxing.

Chapter 8

The double-leg-lift throw

The double-leg-lift is a very effective throw that is a personal favourite of mine. It does not require you to turn your back on the opponent and it can often take them completely by surprise. The throw is found in most forms of wrestling and it is also widely used in judo and jujitsu where it is referred to as 'Morotegari'. The double-leg-lift also appeared in Gichin Funakoshi's book *Rentan Goshin Karate Jutsu* where it is given the name of 'Kusariwa' (Chain Ring). The text tells us that the throw is taken from Passai (Bassai-Dai) kata, or 'Bal Sae' as it is known in the Korean systems. There can also be little doubt that the throw will have also played a part in the early days of boxing. However, because the throw involves taking hold of the opponent's legs its use was outlawed in 1743 due to the introduction of Jack Broughton's rules.

Figure 1

As the opponent reaches forward in an attempt to secure a grip, deflect their arms upward (this being the purpose of the 'double head block' in Passai kata). Throwing the opponent's arms upward in this way will make you less vulnerable to being caught or choked on your way in (**Figure 1**). Lunge forward with your right leg and drop your body downward. Your head should be to the side of the opponent and your shoulder

Figure 2

Figure 3

Figure 4

Figure 5

Figure 6

should be driven into their body. Seize the back of the opponent's legs (**Figure 2**). Continue to drive your shoulder into the opponent as you pull backwards and upwards with both hands. This will take the opponent's feet out from underneath them and cause them to land heavily on their back (**Figure 3**). As soon as the opponent lands, be sure to regain an upright position. If the situation demands it, the opponent's groin is very vulnerable to being kicked due to the fact you have control over both of their legs. Be aware that when you release the opponent's legs you are vulnerable to being kicked if you remain close and inline with the opponent.

If your opponent's back leg is so far away that you can't pick up both legs at once, you could scoop up the leg closest to you, push forward and reap out their supporting leg (see inner reaping throw). Once you have lifted the first leg, it is also possible to push forwards in order to get close enough to grab the opponent's supporting leg (**Figure 4**). You should then lift and pull the other leg in order to execute the throw.

A variation of the double-leg-lift throw is to seize the opponent around the tops of their legs and interlock your hands (not your fingers!) (**Figure 5**). Straighten your legs in order to lift the opponent's feet off the floor (**Figure 6**). Quickly twist to your right whilst swinging your opponent's feet to the left. Release your grip and let the opponent fall to the ground (**Figure 7**).

Figure 7

Chapter 9

The outer-reaping throw

The outer-reaping throw is one of the easiest and most effective throws to apply. It appears in most martial arts (the older versions of them, if not their modern offspring) and its big advantage is that it does not require you to turn your back on your opponent. The outer-reaping throw is commonly used in judo and jujitsu where it is referred to as 'Osotogari'. It has been said that the original jujitsu technique was designed to make use of the spurs worn by samurai horsemen, and the area left unguarded at the back of the calf by samurai armour. A samurai would take his foot past his opponent's leg before driving the spur attached to the back of his heel into his opponent's calf muscle. The outer-reaping throw used in jujitsu today is sometimes thought of as being the 'training version' of the original samurai technique.

A variation of this throw was also used in boxing (before throws were outlawed) which was called 'back-heeling'. The boxer would position his foot behind his opponent's leg and then drive forward so that the opponent would fall. As part of the technique, the boxer would drop his entire weight onto his opponent. The injured opponent would then be dragged to his corner by his seconds and would have a set time (normally around thirty seconds) to make it back to a line in the centre of the ring that was referred to as 'the scratch'. If he did not make it, then the thrower would be declared the winner. Using throws in this way was not uncommon in the days of bare-knuckle boxing. Incidentally, some say that the line in the boxing ring is where the modern expression of 'not up to scratch' (meaning 'unsuitable' or 'substandard') comes from.

The outer-reaping throw is executed as follows. From a clinch, apply a claw-hand attack to the opponent's face. Push up onto the opponent's chin as the fingers are pushed into the opponent's eyes (obviously, this opening technique should only

Figure 1

Figure 2

Figure 3

be used in high-risk situations). At the same time, pull the opponent's arm downwards and to the left. This will break the opponent's balance by forcing them to lean to one side. The majority of the opponent's weight will now be on their right leg (**Figure 1**). Take your body past the opponent and position your right leg behind the opponent's lead leg (**Figure 2**). Continue to push on the opponent's chin and reap your right leg backward in order to complete the throw (**Figure 3**). Once the opponent's balance has been completely broken, be sure to get the reaping leg back on to the floor as quickly as possible.

Chapter 10

The inner-reaping throw

This throw is very similar to the preceding technique. As is suggested by the name of this throw, the main difference is that the opponent's leg is now reaped from the inside. The Japanese name for this throw is 'Ouchigari'.

Drive your head from left to right and strike the opponent's jaw (**Figure 1**). Knee the opponent in the groin (**Figure 2**). Take your foot between your opponent's legs so that your leg is directly behind their lead leg. At this point the back of your calf should be in line with the rear of the opponent's calf (**Figure 3**). Push forward with your arms as you reap backwards, in an arcing fashion, with your lead leg (**Figure 4**). Be

Figure 1

Figure 2

Figure 3

Figure 4

Figure 5

Figure 6

Figure 7

sure to get your foot back onto the floor as quickly as possible.

A variation of this throw is to use the inner-reaping motion to take out the opponent's supporting leg when you have lifted or caught their other leg. This version of the throw is commonly used in karate and taekwondo when the opponent's kicking leg has been caught (**Figure 5**). To use this version of the throw offensively from grappling range, reach downward, take hold of the back of the opponent's leg and lift it up (**Figure 6**). Hitch forward, place your right leg behind the opponent's leg and reap it out as before (**Figure 7**). Reaching down and lifting the leg, before reaping the supporting leg out, is a highly effective and very accessible technique (definitely one of my favourites!).

Chapter 11

The winding throw

The winding throw, or 'standing arm roll' as it is sometimes called, is a very popular wrestling throw. This throw is also used in jujitsu and judo where it goes under the name of 'Makikomi'. The main problem with this throw is that it is very likely that you will end up on the floor with your opponent. If you do fall to the ground, the fact that you will land on top of the opponent can give you an advantage (if the fight is one-on-one and you're a competent ground fighter). The winding throw was used in this way in one of the early UFC (Ultimate Fighting Championship) events. A judoka used the winding throw against a Thai-boxer, and upon landing on top of him delivered a barrage of dropping elbow strikes to the Thai-boxer's skull, knocking him out cold. In real situations we should never deliberately seek a ground-fight, and the winding throw can be executed in such a way that the thrower is more likely to remain vertical.

Deliver an elbow strike to the side of the opponent's jaw (**Figure 1**). Step past the opponent's right leg with your right leg as you feed your striking arm under the opponent's armpit. It is very important that you use your other arm to keep the opponent's arm as close to your body as possible (**Figure 2**). Hug the opponent's

Figure 1

Figure 2

Figure 3   Figure 4

arm in close to you and sharply turn your body. This will pull the opponent over your leg and onto the floor (**Figure 3**). It is important to note that once the opponent's balance is completely broken, you should release the grip with your right arm so that you are not dragged to the ground with the opponent. This version of the throw is found in Passai/Bassai-Dai/Bal Sae kata, where it is often mislabelled as a 180-degree turn and block.

The more common version of this throw involves taking the arm over the top of the opponent's arm. This version has greater momentum, but it is more difficult to release the opponent as they fall. Hence, the over-arm version is more likely to end up with both parties on the floor. Deliver an elbow strike to the opponent's jaw-line as before. Continue the motion of the elbow strike so that your arm is taken over the top of the opponent's arm. Pull the opponent's arm towards

Figure 5

your body as you begin to turn. Take your right foot past your opponent's right foot as your arm drops down and clamps the opponent's arm to your body (**Figure 4**). Drop your body weight and continue to turn in order to take the opponent over your leg and onto the floor. If you should be dragged to the ground with your opponent, you will land on top of them, which could easily damage their ribcage (**Figure 5**). You should then strike the opponent and quickly regain your feet. Although it is unlikely to be the favoured option, the possibility of attacking the elbow joint also exists in this position (**Figure 6**).

Figure 6

Chapter 12

The tackle

The tackle is a relatively simple technique that is often used in mixed martial arts tournaments as a way to take the opponent to the ground. When a ground fight is actively being sought, the tackle is a very effective way of ensuring one. However, in a real fight it is very unwise to actively seek a ground fight! It becomes more difficult to flee and you are very vulnerable to the strikes of your assailant's accomplices. In live situations, the tackle is best used when you are already down whilst the opponent is still upright.

Figure 1

The opponent has knocked you to your knees. Push forwards with your legs as your arms begin to encircle the opponent's legs (**Figure 1**). Secure a tight grip around your opponent's legs as you continue to drive forwards (**Figure 2**). Once the opponent has hit the floor you should quickly stand up.

It is also possible to tackle the opponent to the floor by seizing a single leg. The opponent lifts their leg in preparation for a stamp kick (**Figure 3**). Push the leg past your head with both of your arms as you roll towards the

Figure 2

opponent (**Figure 4**). The primary defensive movement here is the roll inside the effective range of the stamp kick. The covering of the head is a secondary action because without the roll the stamp will go straight through the arms and hit you

Figure 3

Figure 4

Figure 5

Figure 6

anyway. Grab the opponent's rear leg as you rotate your body so that you are straight on to the opponent. Your shoulder should be pushed against the opponent's knee (**Figure 5**). Pull on the opponent's ankle and push your shoulder forwards to lock the opponent's knee joint and tackle them to the floor (**Figure 6**). As before, as soon as the opponent hits the floor you should stand up.

The tackle appears in Kushanku/Kanku-Dai/Kosokun/ Kongsangoon kata and is shown in the appendix at the back of this book.

Chapter 13

The shoulder-wheel throw

The shoulder-wheel throw is one of the most spectacular and potentially painful throws. As is suggested by its name, the shoulder-wheel involves taking the opponent over your shoulders and onto the floor. The opponent is lifted much higher in the air than they are on other throws, and what goes up … must come down! This means that the opponent is likely to have a much harder landing, but it also means that greater skill and strength are required to get the opponent into that position. The shoulder-wheel is referred to as 'kataguruma' in the Japanese martial arts (judo, karate, jujitsu etc) – kataguruma being Japanese for 'shoulder wheel'. In western wrestling systems this throw is most often referred to as 'the fireman's carry'. This name comes from the very similar way in which firemen lift people onto their shoulders in order to move them away from danger. However, firemen generally don't continue the motion of the lift in order to effect a throw!

With regards to karate, taekwondo etc, this throw is most notably found in Wanshu kata. The kata is also known as 'Enpi' in Shotokan karate and 'Eun Bee' in the Korean systems. Wanshu was a Chinese envoy who was sent to the Tomari district of Okinawa in 1683. The kata is said to be a record of Wanshu's fighting methods which were based on Shaolin temple white crane kung-fu. The shoulder-wheel throw can be found towards the end of the kata.

Deliver a hammer-fist strike to the opponent's groin (**Figure 1**). Take your lead leg forwards and pass your striking arm through the opponent's legs. As you do so, pull on the opponent's arm so that

Figure 1

Figure 2

Figure 3

Figure 4

Figure 5

they lean forwards. The strike to the groin is also likely to make the opponent bend forwards. At this point your head should be to the side of the opponent's body (**Figure 2**). Continue to pull the opponent onto your shoulders as you lift with the other arm. At the same time straighten your legs so that the opponent is lifted onto your shoulders (**Figure 3**). From here, you can continue the motion to throw the opponent to the side (**Figure 4**), or you can drop your head and throw the opponent to the front (**Figure 5**).

It is also possible to apply this throw by dropping down onto your knees. Strike the opponent in the groin as before. Drop down and take your lead leg between your opponent's legs. Turn so that you are facing to the side and your lead arm is wrapped around the back of the opponent's leg. Keep your back straight as you pull the opponent's arm, and lift their leg, so that they are loaded onto your shoulders (**Figure 6**). Continue the motion to take the opponent over your shoulders and onto the floor (**Figure 7**).

Another way to load the opponent onto your shoulders is to scoop the lead leg.

Figure 6

Figure 7

Figure 9

Figure 8

This technique is found at the end of Kushanku kata ('Kanku-Dai' in Shotokan karate, 'Kosokun' in Shito-Ryu karate and 'Kongsangoon' in Korean). Turn to the side and take your arm underneath the opponent's lead leg. Lift the opponent's arm just above your head as you step across (**Figure 8**). Pull the opponent's arm downwards so that they are loaded onto your shoulders. At this point your legs should be bent, and your spine should be straight (**Figure 9**). Straighten your legs to lift the opponent into the air.

Figure 10

You can then dump the opponent onto the floor in whatever direction is appropriate. In Kushanku kata the opponent is thrown to the rear (**Figure 10**).

Chapter 14

What if it all goes wrong?

As I mentioned earlier in this book, in the rough and tumble of a live fight there is a good chance that you may fall to the ground with your opponent when executing a throw. This is mainly because the opponent will hold onto you with all their might in an attempt to stay on their feet. It is for this reason that throws work best when they follow a strike. An effective strike will disorientate the opponent and ensure that they will not have the presence of mind to seize you. However, things don't always go to plan. It is important that you know what to do should you end up falling to the ground with your opponent, and even more important to know what to do if you hit the ground alone.

The ground is not somewhere you want to be in a real fight. A ground fight makes it much harder to escape due to your vastly reduced mobility. You are also very vulnerable to the kicks of your opponent's accomplices whilst on the floor. In today's society, fights are rarely one-on-one for any length of time. Even 'spectators' to the fight may decide to get involved if they feel they can get away with a 'free shot'. If you are in an isolated area, with no chance of immediate escape, and you are a good ground fighter, then it could be argued that opting for a ground fight might be a workable strategy. Opting to go to the ground is very common in the mixed martial arts tournaments of today. It was also a strategy sometimes employed in the bare-knuckle boxing matches of the past. However, these are examples from sport. Very tough sports maybe, but still sports. Real fighting is not a sport, and in the vast majority of situations you don't want to end up fighting on the ground.

Ground fighting is to the martial artist what crash-landing is to an aeroplane pilot. You definitely need to know how to do it … but it's never something you choose to do, and all your other skills should be geared towards avoiding it at all costs. In

Figure 1

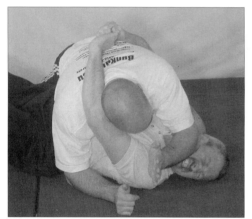

Figure 2

Figure 3

this chapter we will look at regaining our feet should we fall to the ground whilst executing a throw.

In real fights, time spent on the ground must be kept to an absolute minimum. If the fight should go to the ground, the number one priority should be to get back to your feet. If you were the instigator of the throw, it is more likely that you will land in a favourable position. You are more likely to land on top, and the fact that you have landed on the opponent may disorientate them enough to allow you to stand up. If the opponent has the presence of mind to secure a strong grip, you will need to weaken the opponent so that they cannot stop you from standing back up. There are essentially three ways to weaken the opponent whilst on the ground: striking, grabbing (including gouging) and biting. We will look at striking first.

When fighting on the ground you will be unable to get much body weight into your strikes because of your limited movement and close proximity to your opponent. It is here the elbows come into their own. An effective way to elbow the opponent on the ground is to first place the palm of your hand onto the opponent's face and push downward. This will allow you to locate and limit the movement of the opponent's head (**Figure 1**). Quickly move your hand away as you drop your elbow onto the opponent's head (**Figure 2**). You should then repeat the action until the opponent releases their grip. As soon as they do, you should quickly regain your feet. From the position shown, you can also deliver elbows to the opponent's floating ribs. It is also possible to use dropping elbows to the face if the opponent should grab you around the back (**Figure 3**). If you have more room, because the opponent's grip has started to weaken, or if they have grabbed your clothing, you could now use punches or open-handed strikes (**Figure 4**). As before, you should repeatedly strike the opponent until you can stand back up.

Figure 4

The three main targets for gouges/ grabs are the eyes (**Figure 5**), the throat (**Figure 6**) and the testicles (**Figure 7**). These areas are very weak on all men, regardless of their physical size and strength. They are also relatively easy to attack, and that is why they are favoured. However, attacking these areas can cause serious damage to the opponent and their use is only justifiable in extreme situations. Attacks to these areas will cause a great deal of pain and there is a good chance the opponent will release their grip as they try to move your hand away from the area under attack.

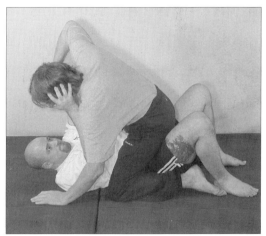

Figure 5

There are other, less dangerous areas that can be effectively gouged/ grabbed. Pushing upward on the base of the nose is very painful (**Figure 8**). As a variation, it is also possible to insert your fingers into the opponent's nostrils. Seizing the flesh on the inside of the opponent's thigh is also very painful. In fact, gripping and scratching the opponent just about anywhere on their body can be a useful part of your 'get to

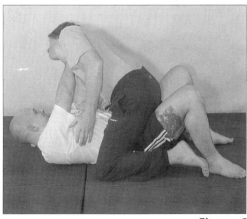

Figure 6

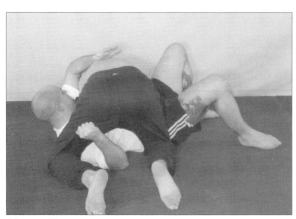

Figure 7

Figure 8

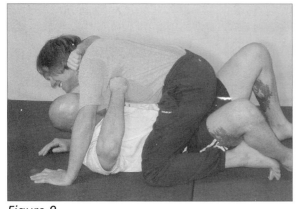

Figure 9

your feet' strategy. One gouge point that causes no permanent damage is the area between the muscles of the chest and back on the side of the ribcage, just under the armpit. Digging in hard with a single knuckle and then raking the knuckle up and down can be very painful (**Figure 9**). The danger with this point is that its effects vary from person to person. It's also worth remembering that the effects of this and other 'nerve points' can be seriously reduced if the opponent is drunk or on drugs. The point is still worth knowing however.

A highly effective, brutal, very unpleasant and extremely unhygienic way of getting to your feet is biting. As I write this, I know there will be some who will read the last sentence and feel that biting an opponent is simply not acceptable. I can understand these reservations, and I would never recommend that you use biting in anything but the most dire of circumstances. However, I maintain that biting is a legitimate method. As martial arts instructors we have a moral duty to teach our students to defend themselves effectively. A small person may find it difficult to fend off a violent physically stronger assailant if they were to 'play by the rules'. However, if they do find themselves overwhelmed, it is possible that they may be able to secure their safety with a well-placed bite. For those who remain adamant that biting is always unacceptable, I'd ask you to consider if you'd still say that if it was your own daughter or wife who had to bite an attacker in order to prevent herself from being assaulted? Certainly it would be morally questionable to bite lumps out of an opponent in a 'square go' (and let's not forget the possible legal issues if such action is not justified). But if biting was the only way for someone to avoid a serious assault, then we shouldn't discount the method. A bite to just about anywhere on the opponent's body is likely to distract them enough to help you to stand back up.

If you are training for real situations, then your ground fighting practise should predominately revolve around the regaining of an upright position. As we covered in Chapter 2, an exercise that will help you to develop some of the required skills is to have your practise partner pin you on the ground. You are then given a minute in which to regain your feet. If you should regain your feet within the minute, you should instantly lie back down, your partner will pin you again, and repeat the exercise until the minute is completed. It should be remembered that spending even a few seconds on the floor is not advisable.

Even worse than ground fighting is when you are on the floor and the opponent is upright. This may be because the opponent has cleanly thrown you, knocked you to the floor or because they have regained their feet and you have not. You are obviously in a very vulnerable position and in all honesty your chances of getting back up unscathed are not good. Your immediate aim should still be to get to your feet as soon as possible. However, it is very important to get up the right way or you will leave yourself very vulnerable to attack.

Figure 10

Figure 11

Figure 12

The first thing you should try to do is to point your feet towards the opponent (**Figure 10**). This keeps your head as far away from the opponent as possible. Notice how one leg is over the top of the other. The position of the legs ensures that the groin is not open to attack. You should use your bottom leg and arm to pivot yourself around on the side of your hip so that your feet remain pointing at the opponent. If the opponent comes close enough you should kick out at their shins and knees with your top leg (**Figure 11**). You should endeavour to shuffle backwards at every opportunity. When you have gained sufficient distance from the opponent, you should quickly get up. It is vitally important that you do not get up with your head towards the opponent because that will leave you very vulnerable to the opponent's kicks (**Figure 12**). Shuffle backwards and start to rise as shown (**Figure 13**). You should then quickly move away from the opponent in order to regain an upright position (**Figure 14**).

If you are on the floor and there are multiple opponents, you are in big trouble! Your only option will be to try to get back up whilst using your arms to cover your head. There is no 'good way' to deal with this situation; you are guaranteed to take a great deal of punishment. Your only hope, aside from others coming to your rescue, is to fight tooth and nail with as much ferocity and aggression as you can muster.

In combat it is important to always have a back-up plan. Should a throw not work as planned, and you do end up on the ground, you must know what to do in order to get back onto your feet as quickly as possible. Most importantly of all, it is vital that you get plenty of quality practise so that it all becomes second nature.

Figure 13

Figure 14

Chapter 15

Conclusion

The way in which the martial arts have evolved has seen them become more and more specialised. 'Grappling arts' now exclusively grapple, and 'striking arts' now concentrate solely on striking. The throws that we have covered in this book were once regarded as a standard part of the 'striking arts'. It is only in relatively recent times that the practise and use of these throws has been abandoned. The arts of boxing, karate, taekwondo etc have always placed the emphasis on striking, but originally basic grappling skills were also practised to back up the striking methods should the opponent get in close.

Today, many martial artists train to defeat practitioners of their own art in rule-bound competition, which needs differing skills to those required for self-defence. Modern sporting rules forbid the use of grappling techniques, and because such techniques are no longer required in the sporting environment they are rarely practised. However, if effective and pragmatic self-defence skills are your aim, then you should definitely include the methods of the older version of your art in your training.

For self-defence purposes, it is not necessary to know many different types of throw. Nor is it necessary to acquire the skill level needed to outwrestle a trained grappler in competition. What you do need are a handful of basic, solid throws that you have practised and made your own. You should never opt to grapple with an assailant in real situations. Your first option should be to avoid the situation altogether. Failing that, you should try to escape. When conflict can in no way be avoided, you should pre-emptivly strike your assailant and then instantly flee. If your first strike does not enable you to escape, you should strike the assailant until the opportunity to run away presents itself. It is only when the assailant has latched onto you, and one of your strikes has provided the ideal

*Group photo – Back row left to right:
Paul Cartmell, Craig Strickland, Fred Moore,
Jim Hopkins, Gary Herbert, Murray Denwood.
Front row: Iain Abernethy (author) and
Peter Skillen (photographer)*

opportunity, that the use of throws should be considered.

The older versions of the martial arts did not consider training outcomes such as physical fitness or sporting glory. Their only aim was the defeat of an opponent in real combat (civilian or military). It is for this main reason that the older arts are much more complete than the modern ones. Whilst the older arts are more complete, they are not as sophisticated as their modern counterparts. For example, it would be foolish in the extreme to compare the basic throws of boxing, karate etc with the highly sophisticated and refined throws of Olympic wrestling or modern judo. However, just because the older methods of the various arts are basic does not mean they are ineffective. It should be remembered that for self-defence purposes basic is the order of the day. It is only when we move away from self-defence towards mutual confrontation/ competition (as many of the modern arts have done) that the more sophisticated and complex methods are really needed.

It is hoped that this book has helped increase your understanding of the 'forgotten' throws of the striking arts, and reintroduce these methods into your training. I'd like to finish by thanking you for purchasing this book and taking the time to read it. Your support of my endeavours is greatly appreciated.

Iain Abernethy

Appendix

Examples from the forms/katas

In this section we are going to briefly look at how some of the throws shown in this book are recorded within the forms/ katas. The whole purpose of a form is to record the key techniques and combative principles of its creator (or sometimes the teacher of the form's creator). As we have already discussed, the martial arts were originally much more broad-based than they are today, and the majority of the forms were developed to record the original art. Hence, it stands to reason that the traditional forms will contain the full range of martial techniques (strikes, locks, chokes, strangles, throws etc). It should also be remembered that the majority of the modern forms are based upon the movements of the traditional forms, so they are also likely to contain some of the older methods (although this is sometimes by default due to the incorrectly perceived purpose of the movement).

One of the problems we face as modern practitioners is the misleading labels that are often attached to the techniques. For example, the cross-buttocks throw appears in a number of karate forms, but it is almost always referred to as something like 'a turning lower block' etc. There are many reasons for this mislabelling, but one of the main ones is that many strikers tend to see everything as strikes, or defences against strikes, due to their lack of exposure to other methods.

We will now have a look at a few examples of throws, both as they appear in the forms and how they would look when applied, which is often slightly different in appearance because of the 'mess' of combat. The aim of this section is to act as 'food for thought' and to encourage you to look for similar movements in your own forms. For a detailed description on how to perform the throws, I'd ask you to refer to the relevant chapter. For a more detailed look at how the forms record practical fighting techniques, I'd ask you to consult my books *Karate's Grappling Methods* and *Bunkai-Jutsu: The Practical Application of Karate Kata*, or my videos on the subject (details at the end of the book). As a final comment, it is important to understand that all of the throws shown throughout this book are found in many different katas and forms. However, only single examples are given here. This is not meant to suggest that the throws shown only appear in the kata that has been named.

Example 1

The cross-buttocks throw is found in Pinan/Heian/Pyung Ann 5. The performance of the 'lower block' maps out the direction in which the arms are to be moved.

Figure 1 – Pull the arm in

Figure 1A – Seize the opponent's arm and pull them in

Figure 2 – Turn into horse stance and perform 'lower block'

Figure 2A – Rotate and execute a cross-buttocks throw

Example 2

The hip throw is found in Pinan/Heian/Pyung Ann 3. The positions of the arms shown in figure three represent the conclusion of the throw.

Figure 3 – Step up with right leg, turn 180° and rotate arms

Figure 3A – Step up and rotate opponent over hips

Example 3

The double leg lift is found in Passai/Bassai-Dai/Bal Sae. The purpose of this movement is mentioned in Gichin Funakoshi's book *Rentan Goshin Karate Jutsu* and a version of the technique is also shown in *Karate-do Kyohan*.

Figure 4 – 'Double hammer-fist'

Figure 4A – Double-leg-lift throw

Example 4

A version of the 'fireman's carry' can be found in Kushanku/
Kanku-Dai/Kosokun/Kongsangoon.

Figure 5 – Turn and take arms to the side

Figure 5A – Step in and scoop the opponent's leg

Figure 6 – 'Double block'

Figure 6A – Load the opponent onto your shoulders

Figure 7 – 'Double outer block'

Figure 7A – Throw

Example 5

The sweep can be found in Naihanchi/Tekki/Chul Ghi.

Figure 8 – 'Reinforced block' and raise foot

Figure 8A – Rotate the opponent's arms and sweep their lead leg

Figure 9 – Turn and 'block'

Figure 9A – Push the opponent completely off balance

Example 6

The tackle can be found in Kushanku/Kanku-Dai/ Kongsangoon.

Figure 10 – Drop to the floor

Figure 10A – Tackle the opponent

Example 7

The winding throw can be found in Passai/Bassai-Dai/Bal Sae.

Figure 11 – 180° turn and 'block'

Figure 11A – Take your leg past the opponent and turn to execute a winding throw

Example 8

A turning version of the neck throw can be found in Kushanku/
Kanku-Dai/Kosokun/Kongsangoon.

*Figure 12 – Pull the
arm in*

*Figure 12A – Trap the
opponent's head
between your forearm
and biceps*

*Figure 13 – Step around
with back foot*

*Figure 13A – Step
around whilst pulling
on the opponent's arm*

*Figure 14 – Execute
'hammer-fist' strike*

*Figure 14A – Continue
to turn in order to take
the opponent to the
floor*

Books
& Videos

Karate's Grappling Methods

This heavily illustrated book takes a detailed look at the grappling techniques of karate. Topics covered include: Understanding kata and bunkai; The role of grappling in self-defence; Close-range strikes; Throws and takedowns; Ground-fighting holds; Chokes and strangles; Arm-bars; Leg and ankle locks; Neck-wrenches; Finger-locks; Wrist-locks; Fighting dirty?; Combinations and Live grappling drills.

"*At long last, a credible and marvellous book on the application of karate kata! And not one that skims the surface looking for frills and thrills, succeeding to entertain but failing abysmally to prepare one for a real, in your face encounter. Rather this book is an in-depth, thoughtful and thought-provoking examination of possibly the deadliest of arts. Karate's Grappling Methods is a great and inspired book.*" Geoff Thompson, world-renowned self-protection expert and best-selling author

ISBN 0 9538932 0 0
246 x 189mm
192 pages
Over 380 illustrations
£15.99 Paperback (+ £2.50 P&P)
Rep. of Ireland & Europe + £4.00 P&P,
    Rest of the World + £5.50 P&P

Available from all good bookstores or direct from NETH Publishing.

Bunkai-Jutsu:
The Practical Application of Karate Kata

Bunkai-Jutsu is the analysis of the karate katas and their application in real combat. It is also the title of this pioneering book by Iain Abernethy. The fighting applications of the karate katas (forms) is one of the most fascinating – and sadly misunderstood – aspects of karate practise. Bunkai-Jutsu provides the reader with the information they need to unlock the 'secrets' of kata and to begin practising karate as the complete and realistic combat art that it was intended to be! This ground-breaking and often controversial book provides a detailed analysis of the combative concepts and principles upon which the katas are based. This book is essential reading for all those who want to understand the real meaning of kata.

"Bunkai-Jutsu explains every aspect of the katas and their application in real combat." Doug James, 7th Dan

"No martial arts library is complete without Bunkai-Jutsu. Iain Abernethy has shown us the real beauty of karate with his innovative and pioneering work." Geoff Thompson, 6th Dan karate, self-protection expert and best-selling author

ISBN 0 9538932 1 9
246 x 189mm
240 pages
Over 235 illustrations
£17.99 Paperback (+ £2.50 UK P&P)
Rep. of Ireland & Europe + £4.00 P&P,
    Rest of the World + £5.50 P&P

Available from all good bookstores or direct from NETH Publishing.

Karate's Grappling Methods Videos

See the karate katas brought to life with these professionally produced videos. Both videos provide in-depth instruction on the highly effective close-range techniques and concepts recorded within the karate katas.

   (The KGM book and videos contain many differing techniques in addition to supporting one another.)

Karate's Grappling Methods Video Vol 1

Close-range strikes, Neck-cranks, Arm-locks, Wrist-locks and Leg-locks

Running time: approx 50 minutes
£16.50 inc UK Postage & Packing
(Rep of Ireland & Europe + £1.50,
   Rest of the World + £3.00)

Karate's Grappling Methods Video Vol 2

Throws and takedowns, Chokes and strangles, Finger-locks, Ground-fighting holds, Keeping it simple, Nerve points, Live sparring.

Running time: approx 50 minutes
£16.50 inc UK Postage & Packing
(Rep of Ireland & Europe + £1.50,
   Rest of the World + £3.00)

Bunkai-Jutsu Videos

Bunkai-Jutsu is the analysis of the karate katas and their application in real combat. These high-quality tapes reveal the effective fighting applications recorded in the katas. The application of every single move is shown complete with instruction on the style variations. These videos are a must for all karateka – regardless of style – who wish to practise karate as a complete and effective combat system.

Bunkai-Jutsu Vol 1: The Pinan/Heian Series

Volume one covers the applications of the Pinan/Heian (peaceful mind) series. The great Anko Itsou formulated these katas in the early 1900s. They are a complete system of fighting in their own right and were designed to be a collection of the most effective methods being practised in the Shuri region of Okinawa at that time. This video examines the strikes, locks, throws, chokes, strangles, traps, ground-fighting and combative strategies recorded within the Pinan/Heian series.

Running time: approx 2 Hours
£19.45 inc UK Postage & Packing
(Rep of Ireland & Europe + £1.50,
Rest of the World + £3.00)

Bunkai-Jutsu Vol 2: Naihanchi/Tekki and Passai/ Bassai-Dai

Volume two covers Naihanchi (Tekki) and Bassai-Dai (Passai). Today, Naihanchi/Tekki is often undervalued due to its simplistic appearance. This video shows the highly effective close-range fighting applications of the form and reveals just why the kata was so highly regarded by the masters of old. The second part of the tape covers Passai/Bassai-Dai kata and demonstrates the strikes, throws, takedowns, locks, neck-cranks, chokes, combative strategies etc that have made this form one of the most popular in the history of karate.

Running time: approx 1 hour 30 mins
£19.45 inc UK Postage & Packing
(Rep of Ireland & Europe +£1.50,
Rest of the World +£3.00)

Ordering and contact details

Please make cheques/UK postal orders payable to "NETH Publishing"

Send to:

NETH Publishing, PO Box 38, Cockermouth, Cumbria, CA13 0GS, UK

24-hour credit/debit card hotline:

☎ 01900 829406 (UK)

☎ +44 1900 829406 (International)

For a full list of all NETH Publishing products and to receive our FREE newsletters, please send your name and address to NETH Publishing.

Iain Abernethy can be contacted via the NETH Publishing address or emailed at:

iain@iainabernethy.com

Order on-line at www.iainabernethy.com

www.iainabernethy.com

www.summersdale.com